GW00383178

Saint
Francis
OF ASSISI

DEVOTIONS, PRAYERS & LIVING WISDOM

Saint
Francis
OF ASSISI

Edited by Mirabai Starr

Sounds True, Inc., Boulder, CO 80306

Published 2007
Printed in Canada
ISBN 978-1-59179-628-2
Library of Congress Cataloging-in-Publication Data

Francis, of Assisi, Saint, 1182-1226.
  [Selections. English. 2007]
  Francis of Assisi : devotions, prayers, and living wisdom /
  [translated by] Mirabai Starr.
     p. cm. -- (Devotions, prayers, and living wisdom series ; bk. 1)
     Includes bibliographical references (p. 129).
     ISBN 978-1-59179-628-2 (hardcover)
  1. Spiritual life--Catholic Church--Early works to 1800. 2.
  Spirituality--Catholic Church--Early works to 1800. 3.
  Christian life--Catholic authors--Early works to 1800. I.
  Starr, Mirabai. II. Title. III. Title: Devotions, prayers, and
  living wisdom.

BX2179.F64E5 2007
271'.302--dc22

                                2007031064

For a free catalog of wisdom teachings for the inner life, call
(800) 333-9185 or visit www.soundstrue.com.

Contents

Publisher's Note

ounds True's Devotions, Prayers, and Living Wisdom series began with a desire to offer the essential teachings of great saints, mystics, and spiritual figures in a format that is compatible with meditation and contemplation. Each book contains poems, prayers, songs, and prose written by or in veneration of a figure who has transcended human confusion, and whose wisdom might awaken our own. It is our hope that these books will offer you insight, renewal, and companionship on the spiritual path.

Editor's Note

Before embarking on the journey of compiling materials for this book, I thought of Francis as the Happy Saint. There he stands in gardens everywhere, birds on his shoulders, hands raised in exaltation. And Francis *was* joyful. He did take great delight in creatures and creation, because they reminded him of the awesome grandeur of the Creator.

Along the way, I discovered that Francis also suffered terribly. He endured persecution from the moment he walked away from his father's inheritance to the day he died, leader of a rapidly burgeoning religious order. He was weakened by penances and austerities, wracked by disease and blindness. Revered by thousands in his own lifetime, Francis felt radically alone.

Strangely, rather than being disappointed, I was uplifted by this revelation. If the great Saint Francis was human, as I am human, if he struggled with the familiar issues of health and interpersonal conflict and still raised his heart to praise God, then I, too, have permission to be human and to love the Holy One in my own very human way.

For this collection, I drew from many early accounts of Saint Francis by his original followers, and they carry the romantic flavor of the Middle Ages. I adapted certain anecdotes in my own words, too, distinguished by italics in the text. Certain modern poets contribute their reflections on this timeless wisdom teacher. A list at the back of the book will guide the reader to the various sources from which I drew my selections.

Four chapters arrange the material according to the major themes I identified in the existing body of Francis literature: kinship with the earth and her creatures; the power of faith; the relationship between Saint Francis and his best friend, Saint Clare; and the gifts of holy poverty and voluntary simplicity.

It is my prayer that these devotional writings fill your heart with the wild abandon that set Saint Francis free.

I am deeply grateful for the generous contributions and wise guidance of Father William Hart McNichols, Father David Denny, Tessa Bielecki, Lynn-at-Lama-Foundation, Kaysi Contreras, Sara Morgan, Sarah Jane Freymann, Kelly Notaras, and Haven Iverson.

— Mirabai Starr
June 2007

Opening Prayer

Praise to you,
Saint Francis of Assisi,
brother to the sun and the moon,
to birds and worms, fire and wind.
Your unconditional love of creation
excludes no one.
When you embraced the leper
anything left between you and your God
melted away.

In our habitual grasping,
we have lost the joy of letting go.
Whisper in our ear, Francis.
Let us live your simple wisdom,
and seek not so much to be understood
as to understand,
to be loved as to love.

Thank you.
Amen.

—Mirabai Starr

Introduction

History likes to portray Francis of Assisi as a perfect being, unmoved by the trials that bring the rest of us to our knees. A placid sage who held out his holy hands to the gentle forest creatures while they scurried and swooped and glided to greet him. An innocent child-man who easily slips into the kingdom of heaven while the rest of us grapple outside the gates with our thousand grown-up concerns and responsibilities, failing again and again to meet our lives gracefully.

It is comforting to discover that Francis of Assisi suffered and lamented, lost his temper and forfeited his dignity, rebelled against the rebels and lashed out at the meek. That, like us, he fell again and again. And that he continued to stand up, brush himself off, and recommit his life to God. It is precisely in his humanness that his true sanctity lies; it is in that same essential humanity that we can find a role model for a deeply spiritual life.

Like most great prophets, Francis of Assisi became a saint in spite of himself. The more he tried to disappear into the unifying light of the Divine, the more the Holy One seemed to raise him up as a shining example of what is meant by the phrase "Love one another."

Eight centuries after his death, this humble Italian sage is the most popular saint in the world. Saint Francis dissolves the boundaries between believers and doubters, leaps over the fence that divides religious traditions to penetrate the heart and inflame the imagination in every culture and across the centuries. Who doesn't love this gentle, joyful saint, a being who preaches to the birds with one hand and blesses lepers with the other?

Francis of Assisi was born in 1182 and died in 1226. In his 44 years on the planet, he managed to reform the entire Roman Catholic Church—not through revolution and dissent, but through gracious persuasion and his own living example of an authentic gospel life. Francis committed every breath to making the Beatitudes of Jesus Christ a daily reality.

*Blessed are the poor in spirit,
for theirs is the kingdom of heaven.*

Francis dedicated himself to uplifting the wretched
conditions of the poor. He gave up his inherited
wealth and privilege to live among the outcasts,
the marginalized, the struggling, identifying with
them as Jesus identified with them. If Francis
received a half a loaf of bread in his begging bowl,
he divided it among all who were hungry. He
refused all possessions beyond the patched robe
he wore to cover "Brother Body."

*Blessed are those who mourn,
for they shall be comforted.*

Francis understood that great sorrow shatters our
hearts and that only in that shattering can the
light of the Divine come streaming in. Into the
vessel hollowed out by grief and loss, the Holy
One pours his love and fills us to overflowing.

Francis tended to that emptying with boundless lovingkindness. Wherever he perceived suffering, he offered comfort, both in the form of physical relief and spiritual illumination.

Blessed are the meek,
for they shall inherit the earth.

Francis quietly suggested that the lavish materialism of the Church was an impediment to spiritual growth. It is the gentle and not the powerful who will drink from the divine cup. It is the humble who will uncover the divine treasure that lifts the burden of debt for themselves and for all humanity.

Blessed are those who hunger and thirst
for righteousness, for they shall be filled.

Francis inspired his followers to desire the liberation of their brothers and sisters as passionately as they themselves longed to be free. He modeled a spiritual path that combined private, contemplative prayer with active service in the world.

While Francis could easily have become the respected leader of a successful monastic community, removed from the distractions of society, he chose instead to immerse himself in the messy human condition, where he was often reviled as an embarrassment to the high society from which he came. Rather than accept a traditional endowment, Francis and his followers begged in the streets for bread, bricks, and firewood. He tended lepers and cared for orphans. He stood up against oppression wherever he encountered it, but he did so in such a loving way that he posed no obvious threat to the authorities and so managed to convert them to his cause.

Blessed are the merciful,
for they shall obtain mercy.

Francis insisted that, in choosing a life of voluntary poverty and radical simplicity, his followers not criticize those who were not ready for such extreme practices. In an age where communities of bold heretics were hurling accusations of hypocrisy at the Roman Church, Francis embraced and forgave the transgressions of Christendom with the same humility and tenderness with which he treated every individual soul that crossed his path. He invited all who had been rejected by society to take refuge among the Little Brothers and rebuild their inherent dignity in a climate of authentic compassion.

Blessed are the pure in heart,
for they shall see God.

Francis saw the face of the Creator throughout his creation. In the unself-conscious symphony of birdsong, Francis learned how to joyously praise the Holy One. Watching a toddler teeter into his mother's arms, Francis recognized the simple pleasures of house-holding. As he had given these up to follow the most radical teachings of Christ, he sculpted a family of snowpeople to symbolize his sacrifice and make fun of his own longings for human connection. Francis refused to take himself seriously. His childlike wonder in the beauty of the natural world lifted the veils that separated him from a direct encounter with the Divine.

Blessed are the peacemakers,
for they shall be called the Children of God.

Francis was born into a cult of knighthood, in which young men of noble birth were expected to charge off and vanquish their neighbors in an ongoing culture of civil strife. After spending a year as a prisoner of war following one such pointless battle, Francis experienced the futility of violence in every fiber of his being. He exchanged his suit of armor for a trowel to lay mortar and bricks in the restoration of ruined churches. And in place of the classical songs of chivalry he used to perform as a troubadour, Francis picked up two sticks and pantomimed a violin, singing love songs to God in French while his brothers danced in holy intoxication.

*Blessed are those who are
persecuted for righteousness' sake,
for theirs is the kingdom of heaven.*

Francis began and ended his religious vocation the victim of condemnation and rejection.
When he first gave up his life of comfort and
ease and took to the streets to live among the
poor and beg for his most basic needs, the
people of Assisi slammed their doors in his face
and called him crazy. When he began to rebuild
churches and preach a gospel of radical simplicity and unconditional love, they laughed at him.
Gradually yet inexorably, Francis' gentleness
and passion attracted followers, until the small
brotherhood founded on voluntary poverty had
flowered into a complex organization, rife with
internal conflict and misunderstanding, one that
barely resembled Francis' original vision. This
betrayal broke his heart, yet it also opened him
to receive the ultimate gift from Christ: participa-
tion in his Passion through the stigmata.

The full spectrum of Francis' life—from joyful exaltation of the Lord to crushing self-doubt—reflected his living commitment to Christ's teachings of love.

Francesco

His birth name was John—Giovanni, in Italian. Giovanni di Pietro di Bernadone. His father, Pietro di Bernadone, was a wealthy Umbrian cloth merchant and his mother, Pica, was French. After a family trip to France, where the young Giovanni was captivated by the markets and the music, the women and the poetry, his father started to call him Francesco, "the Frenchman." Francis of Assisi.

Francis was groomed for the family business. As a teenager, he was far more interested in romance than in commerce, but his antics fell well within the boundaries of acceptable behavior. He was famous among the youth of Assisi for throwing wild parties, providing a bountiful flow of wine, disappearing with beautiful women into darkened rooms, strolling the city streets till dawn, singing the love songs of the troubadour. It was the beginning of the thirteenth century, and Francis was reared on the medieval myths of gallant knights and noble ladies. His primary ambition was to be adored as a hero.

Until he was captured in a battle with Perugia, and his goals radically shifted. Francis spent a year as a prisoner of war, during which he had ample opportunity to contemplate the superficiality of his privileged life. Into the abyss that opened out of the depths of uncompromising self-inquiry, Francis began to feel the presence of a loving God, a God who called his beloveds into a direct and personal relationship. He began to listen for the divine voice in the silence of his captivity.

When Francis was ransomed by his father, he returned home and fell seriously ill. His parents patiently tended him, but Francis was drawing further and further away from them. His con-genial nature was replaced by a deep stillness that neither friends nor family could penetrate. He was courteous, but distracted, slipping in and out of a fever that began to look increasingly like prayer. Francis was undergoing a spiritual crisis, one that would permanently transfigure the wild youth into a holy sage. He still showed no signs of interest in following in his businessman father's footsteps.

One day, after Francis had begun to recover at last, he went out riding alone in the Umbrian countryside. As he broke through a clearing in the forest, he simultaneously heard the warning sound of a leper's bell and saw the ravaged man appear from behind a tree. It was a cold day, and the leper wore nothing but rags. Francis, who had always been disgusted and frightened by leprosy, leapt off his horse, crossed the clearing, and wrapped his cloak tenderly around the man's bony shoulders. Stunned by his own impulse, Francis looked into the leper's grateful eyes and, his own eyes welling with tears, kissed the man's oozing face.

This was a turning point on Francis' path. What had always been bitter was suddenly sweet. What he had run from now had unspeakable allure. He did not care about being comfortable; he wanted only to give comfort. He was not interested in a full belly when, all around him, people were suffering from starvation. But what exactly could he do to alleviate the suffering of humanity?

He could join with it.

This mission did not begin overnight. First Francis would make a half-hearted effort to please his parents and join his father's trade. But wherever he went and whatever he did, Francis heard the whisper of the Holy One guiding him to a life of loving service.

As he was taking shelter from the summer sun one day in an ancient church outside the city gates, Francis heard the voice of Christ address him from the crucifix on the wall. Christ pointed out that his house was falling into ruin, and he called upon Francis to rebuild it.

This was another turning point. Francis raced home, grabbed handfuls of expensive fabric from his father's storeroom, and sold it far below market price in a neighboring village. Then he donated the money to the bewildered priest at the dilapidated church to finance a full restoration. Pietro, who had tried to practice patience up to this point, broke. He hauled his wayward son before the bishop of Assisi and demanded recompense for what Francis had "stolen" from him.

As Francis stood before the bishop, who was dressed more like a prince than a follower of the barefoot Jesus Christ, and his seething father, and the jeering crowd of citizens, suddenly everything became clear. He did not own anything. Neither his father nor the bishop nor the men and women of Assisi really owned a thing. Everything on earth belonged to the Holy One. How could we do anything but praise the Creator and serve all of creation?

In a burst of wild joy, Francis stripped off his fine clothes and laid them at his father's feet. He renounced his inheritance and embraced a life of radical poverty in solidarity with the people. Naked, he walked away from the only life he had ever known, and he never returned. Ironically, Francis of Assisi was designated the patron saint of merchants by the Catholic Church.

ᗙᗙᗙ The Little Brothers ᗙᗙᗙ

It did not take long for the young men and women of Assisi to investigate their old friend's new life. Once they encountered the sweet contentment and transformational inspiration of Francis' message and practices, they soon began to join him. Word spread far beyond the Umbrian region, and Francis attracted spiritual seekers in droves. Clare of Assisi, a beautiful young woman from a powerful family, dramatically divested herself of wealth and privilege and became one of Francis' most devoted companions.

Unlike other reformers of his time, Francis was not looking for followers. He simply wanted to align his life with what he considered to be the essence of Christ's teachings of love, charity, and poverty. He welcomed everyone who wished to join him in this endeavor, but he did not presume to be their leader. This did not stop people from looking to him as their spiritual master and guide.

As the brotherhood grew, the brothers began to demand that Francis draft some kind of monastic rule. They craved a structure to support them on this wild path they had embarked upon: a name, a code of conduct, a set of practices. Francis jotted down a stark list of guidelines, and in 1210, a small group of companions followed Francis to Rome to ask Pope Innocent III for his approval of the new order, which Francis simply called the Friars Minor, or the Little Brothers. Struck by the purity of Francis' intention and the apparent lack of heretical elements in his vision, the Pope granted their request, but his blessing was verbal and never documented in writing.

Over the centuries, the Franciscan order burgeoned from a band of barefoot visionaries into one of the most powerful branches of the Roman Catholic Church. Even in Francis' own lifetime, the following that flowered around him took on a life of its own, ultimately drifting far from his original ideals, causing its founder deep grief and alienation. Eventually, Francis would feel compelled to step down as official head of the Friars Minor, resulting in a dramatic relaxation of the commitment to poverty.

But the early days of the new order were infused with optimism. The brothers lived joyfully, sleeping beneath the stars or in simple wattle and daub hermitages, wandering the Umbrian landscape, preaching a gospel of unconditional love. In 1212, in response to the influx of women, Francis founded the second order, the Poor Ladies (later to be called the Poor Clares) and appointed his lifetime companion, Clare (Chiara, in Italian), as its head. Unlike the Little Brothers, who were wandering preachers and healers, the Poor Clares lived in an enclosed convent, where their primary practice was contemplative prayer.

Sickened by the increasing violence surrounding the latest wave of the Crusades, Francis set out on a journey to North Africa in 1219, with the intention of converting the Muslims to Christianity through the sheer power of Christ's teachings. The Egyptian sultan, intrigued by the holy reputation of the Christian mystic, allowed Francis to preach to him and his people. Although their encounter did not turn the sultan into a Christian, Malik al-Kamil listened politely to the barefoot friar and affirmed the beauty of his faith before guiding him safely back to the Christian side of the line.

Not all of Francis' followers took monastic vows. Many laypeople, both single and married, were moved to build their lives on the foundation of Francis' teachings by living simply and caring for the poor. As Francis preached to these householders, one of the friars wrote down his sermon, and this became the basis for a rule of life for laypeople. This document gave rise to the third Franciscan order, joining the team of the Friars Minor and the Poor Clares. The Third Order, then, was composed of those who wanted to follow the way St. Francis showed, but were not able or willing to leave the world and join a monastic community.

As the years unfolded, Francis focused more on preaching and prayer and less on the administrative details of his sprawling brotherhood. He was not suited for politics. Yet the politics were heating up. A combination of internal discord and interference from the new pope finally convinced Francis to resign as Minister General of the order. He chose his replacement and retired to his hermitage to draft a formal rule as his final executive act.

In 1224, ravaged by penance and disease, and nearly blind, the forty-two-year-old friar climbed Mount La Verna to spend St. Michael's Lent in solitude and contemplative prayer. He was broken: broken-hearted, broken-bodied. The brotherhood that once consisted of a few companions passionately dedicated to giving everything away and trusting in God now included over 5,000 members throughout Europe and the Holy Land. Many of these new brothers had never laid eyes on their founder, yet took it upon themselves to reform the order, entitling members to receive and use wealth as long as they didn't "own" it. This distinction alienated Francis from his own spiritual family.

On the Feast of the Flowering Cross in 1224, alone in his mountaintop hermitage, Francis received the stigmata, the marks of Christ's wounds on his hands, feet, and sides. He had pleaded with Christ to allow him to directly participate in his suffering and the love that had prompted him to endure it. His beloved Brother Jesus answered his prayer. Francis tried to hide the evidence of his imitation of the divine sacrifice, but rumors of the miracle quickly spread among the people and filled their hearts with awe.

At the end of his life, feeling the presence of Sister Death waiting to receive him, Francis, who had always experienced a sacred intimacy with plants and animals, earth and sky, composed "The Canticle of the Creatures." This most famous of his writings is a hymn in praise of our connectedness to all life. He returned to the Porziuncola to die, the place where the order had first been born. Two years later, Francis of Assisi was canonized as a saint of the Catholic Church. Eight hundred years later, he is known as a saint throughout the world, igniting the imaginations of Christians and atheists, romantics and pragmatists, lovers of nature and advocates for human rights. Francis transcends all limitations with his joyful, humble, incendiary love of God.

ᲦᲐᲘᲔᲚᲘᲝ Joy ᲦᲐᲘᲔᲚᲘᲝ

J n 1980, Pope John Paul II declared Francis of Assisi the patron saint of ecology. Francis took the biblical teaching about man being given dominion over creation and turned it in his gentle hand. Francis taught that God had created human beings as stewards for the rest of his creatures, and for the earth and the elements that sustain us all. Rather than viewing himself as the master of the animals, or nature as an indifferent collection of forces, Francis embraced all created things as his family. He delighted in the smallest details of the Creator's humblest children.

And creation responded in kind. Especially the animals. When Francis preached in the open air, chattering birds became suddenly silent and then resumed their cacophony as soon as he said "Amen." Crickets came tracking through the snow to the window of his cell when Francis recited the midnight prayers in deep winter, shaming the friars who could not bring themselves to rise from their beds. It is said that the animals of the forest surrounding the hermitage where Francis died crowded around his room, singing and barking and howling their lamentations.

One of the most famous accounts about Francis' bond with animals is the story of the Wolf of Gubbio. It happened that a large and ferocious wolf was terrorizing the inhabitants of this mountain town. The creature was starving. At first it slaughtered farm animals, but then it began attacking human beings. No one dared to wander beyond the city gates for fear of being devoured.

When Francis was visiting Gubbio and saw how the people were suffering, he took it upon himself to confront the wolf. That night, the people of the town climbed the city wall to watch as Friar Francis ventured to the edge of the woods. He had hardly advanced ten steps when the wolf leapt out of the forest and ran toward Francis, its teeth bared. Francis held up his hand and made the sign of the cross in the air between them. The wolf stopped in its tracks and closed its mouth.

"Come to me, Brother Wolf," Francis said. And the wolf approached the saint and lay down at his feet like a lamb.

Francis explained that he understood the wolf was suffering from hunger but that it had no right to cause this kind of anguish among the humble citizens of Gubbio. He offered to help make peace between the people and the wolf by convincing the townspeople to feed the wolf every day, in exchange for the wolf's promise to never to hurt anyone again. When Francis asked the wolf for a sign of assent, the animal bowed its head and wagged its tail. Then he turned to the crowd and obtained their vow to uphold their end of the peace pact. He offered himself as bondsman for "Brother Wolf."

From that day onward, the wolf appeared in the town every afternoon, stopping at a different house to be fed. The wolf was gentle and the humans courteous. When the wolf finally died of old age, the people of Gubbio grieved. Its sweetness and patience had been a daily reminder of the holiness of Saint Francis.

For Francis, all things were reflections of the Creator and served as reminders to praise him. The beauty of creation provided constant opportunities for rejoicing. Francis' love of God was so vast that it spilled over and flooded everything he saw and touched. He treated bishops and earthworms with equal courtesy. A fire in the hearth was as likely to send him into rapture as a hymn in the cathedral. More so! He was less kind to himself than he was to the grasshoppers that ravaged his herb garden. He called his body "Brother Ass," and put up with its stubbornness with long-suffering patience rather than true respect.

In the relationship between Brother Francis and Sister Clare, we witness the more vulnerable side of the saint. With Clare, Francis could allow himself to let down, to be nurtured and comforted, to play. A boyish joyousness radiated from his eyes whenever he saw her. Chiara, sister of light, lit up Francesco's heart and made all things right.

He also bore a special love for the infant Jesus. A favorite Francis story unfolds one winter solstice, the deepest, darkest time of the year. The Umbrian landscape was draped in a thick blanket of snow. In a few days, the brothers would celebrate Christmas at Greccio. Francis, exhausted and ill, expressed his longing to honor the Christ child in some special way.

So the brothers constructed a replica of Christ's crib, spread straw on the platform, and fabricated the barnyard animals, the blessed mother, and her holy husband. They painted stars on the backdrop to shine above the humble scene and placed torches everywhere to light the way for the Word of God to fill the flesh of a baby boy.

When Francis was brought in to see the manger, he was overcome by awe at the mystery of the incarnation. He fell to his knees, murmuring private praises. The village people came from their houses to witness the miracle of the incarnation. Christmas hymns rose into the night sky and penetrated the winter air like leaping flames. The rocks and trees bore witness to their simple joy.

୬୬୬୬ Sorrow ୬୬୬୬

But as his vision of a brotherhood based on the radical values of poverty and humility began to crumble, Francis slipped deeper into a dark night of the soul. He knew nothing anymore. All familiar spiritual sensations dried up, and every religious concept evaporated. But Francis did not abandon his faith. He turned his radical values inward. He surrendered to the poverty of feeling nothing. He embraced the ineffable knowledge that comes only with unknowing.

His Beloved was stripping Francis of everything that stood between them. Self-mortification was a flame that ignited the garment of his ego, annihilating his small self so that his true self could fall into the arms of divine union. Francis did his part: emptying the cup of his soul. The Holy One responded by filling Francis' cup with love.

The last six years of Francis' life were marked by physical illness and emotional turmoil. Men he had never met had managed to take control of the brotherhood and betray his most cherished ideals. His eyes filled with pus until he could no longer see anything but shadowy shapes. When Francis recalled Christ's trials, he found consolation in sharing a tiny taste of the divine anguish.

It is Francis of Assisi who introduced the practice of meditating on the Passion of Christ as a means for breaking through to God's unconditional love. But for Francis, this was not simply a religious exercise. His compassion for the suffering of Jesus was so intense that he spent hours weeping bitterly. Some of his companions reported that, long before he went blind, Francis sometimes cried so hard he shed tears of blood.

One day, while Francis was kneeling in the woods, sobbing over the suffering of the crucified Christ, he encountered a man out walking. When the man asked the friar why he was crying, Francis countered by asking how anyone could hold back his tears in the face of such a sacrifice as Jesus made for us. And the man, overcome by the saint's devotion, cried with him.

Francis did not always suffer his challenges cheerfully. Sometimes the frail ascetic raged against the circumstances and the people who defied him. "Who are they," he bellowed, "to snatch my order and my brethren from my hand?" When he visited the Porziuncola one day and found strangers building a stone church on the sacred ground where the brotherhood had first made their home, Francis climbed the roof and began hurling down the tiles with his own hands.

Other times, Francis allowed himself to be thoroughly humiliated without uttering a word of protest. Arriving cold and exhausted at the house of some friars he did not know, he was turned away with curses and blows. Instead of giving in to the temptation of self-righteousness, Francis huddled in the rain and thanked God for the opportunity to share in the divine sorrow. "This," he said, "is perfect joy."

When he stood up before an assembly of thousands of friars, imploring them to be faithful to his beloved Lady Poverty, they mocked him and dismissed him. Francis ended up revising his strict rule of life to make a dozen concessions he never would have dreamed of making at the outset, such as relaxed adherence to Jesus' injunctions against owning property of any kind. But even these did not please his detractors. They replaced the primitive rule with a set of standards that did not even resemble the founding inspiration. It was this severely compromised structure for spiritual formation that finally received papal approval.

Toward the end of his life, as his many illnesses coalesced into a single lethal mass, Francis' closest companions begged him to move to a place where conditions would be more comfortable and conducive to healing. The bishop insisted that Francis come live with him. But the only place Francis was willing to relocate to was a rough hut outside the convent of San Damiano. He wanted to be near Clare, who tended him with loving care and yet honored his commitment to simplicity.

Troubled by his blindness, Francis finally agreed to allow a physician to cauterize his eyes in hopes of restoring his sight. As the doctor plunged a poker into the glowing embers, Francis addressed the flame: "Brother Fire, I have always loved and honored you. Please do not burn me more than I can bear." And the saint did not flinch as the healer scalded the tender flesh around his eyes. The remedy did nothing to improve Francis' vision, but the saint praised God for the miracle of feeling not a trace of pain.

This was St. Francis. He did not intentionally place sorrow over gladness, but when pain filled his cup, he gratefully accepted the opportunity to share a tiny sip of the sacrifice he felt his Lord had made on his behalf. And yet, when the joy bubbled up and overflowed his heart, Francis would not hesitate to leap to his feet, grab two sticks, and play a love song to God on his imaginary violin.

Chapter One

Sister Earth,
Our Mother

༄ Guests of God ༄

now that he has fallen in love with God, Francis recognizes his relatedness to all life. If the creator is his father, then all living things are his sisters and brothers. This connectedness fills him with wild joy, a joy that spills over every vessel of the human experience and flows back into the earth, giving birth to the endless unfolding of creation.

Francis invites everyone to his table, which is God's table:

Each morning, he welcomes Brother Sun with passionate gratitude, because the sun perpetually bears the original light of the Holy One.

He welcomes Brother Fire, who brings comfort to the night.

He welcomes Sister Water, who washes away all iniquities with her power and her purity.

He welcomes his sisters, Moon and Stars,
who brighten the heavens and beckon us home.

He welcomes his brothers, Wind and Storm,
who teach us to cherish the cycles of seasons
that shelter all creation.

He welcomes Sister Earth and calls her
Mother, blessing the countless reminders she
offers of the infinite beauty of the Holy One,
thanking her for her abundant nourishment of
our bodies and our souls.

Francis welcomes rocks to this table, because
Christ is his rock. He welcomes flowers and
herbs, whose color and sweetness inspire us to
sing God's praises. He welcomes fish and worms,
crickets and larks, each of whom has its own
special way of praising God. He protects lambs,
because his beloved Brother Jesus is the Lamb of
God. He allows only dead limbs to be harvested
for firewood so that every living tree can con-
tinue its reach toward heaven.

He even welcomes Sister Death—maybe
Sister Death especially—who will receive us one
day in her tender embrace and deliver us into
the waiting arms of the Holy One.

And yet, though he has no doubt that the life beyond this life is Life Everlasting, Francis does not consider his corporeal existence to be a form of exile, but a reminder of God's lovingkindness.

The more saintly Saint Francis grows, the more human he becomes. His love of creation keeps him close to the earth, where he rejoices in the simple yet unutterably holy gift of being a man, a man connected to other men and to women, to earth and sky, to forest and village and river and sea, to the tiny ant and the majestic eagle, to winter snowfall and the promise of spring sleeping beneath it.

Canticle of the Sun

Most high, all powerful sweet Lord,
yours is the praise, the glory, and the honor
and every blessing.

Be praised, my Lord,
for all your creatures,
and first for brother sun,
who makes the day bright and luminous.

And he is beautiful and radiant
        with great splendor,
he is the image of you, Most High.

Be praised, my Lord,
for sister moon and stars,
in the sky you have made them
        brilliant and precious and beautiful.

Be praised, my Lord, for brother wind
and for the air both cloudy and serene
        and every kind of weather,
through which you give nourishment
        to your creatures.

Saint Francis of Assisi

Be praised, my Lord, for sister water,
who is very useful and humble
and precious and chaste.

Be praised, my Lord, for brother fire,
through whom you illuminate the night.
And he is beautiful and joyous
and robust and strong.

Be praised, my Lord,
for our sister, mother earth,
who nourishes us and watches over us
and brings forth various fruits
with colored flowers and herbs.

Be praised, my Lord,
for those who forgive through your love,
and bear sickness and tribulation;

blessed are those who endure in peace,
for they will be crowned by you, Most High.

Be praised, my Lord,
for our sister, bodily death,
from whom no living thing can escape.

Sister Earth, Our Mother

Blessed are those whom she finds
    doing your most holy will,
for the second death cannot harm them.

Praise and bless my Lord
    and give thanks to him and serve him
with great humility.

— St. Francis of Assisi

When I Returned
From Rome

A
bird took flight.
And a flower in a field whistled at me
as I passed.

I drank
from a stream of clear water.
And at night the sky untied her hair and I fell asleep
clutching a tress
of God's.

When I returned from Rome, all said,
"Tell us the great news,"

and with great excitement I did:"A flower in a field whistled,
and at night the sky untied her hair and
I fell asleep clutching a
sacred tress . . ."

— In the spirit of St. Francis of Assisi
Daniel Ladinsky

My sister birds, you owe much to God, and you must always and in every place give praise to him;

For he has given you freedom to wing through the sky and he has clothed you . . .

You neither sow nor reap and God feeds you and gives you rivers and fountains for your thirst, and mountains and valleys for shelter, and tall trees for your nests.

And although you neither know how to spin or weave, God dresses you and your children, for the Creator loves you greatly and he blesses you abundantly.

Therefore . . . always seek to praise God.

— from *The Little Flowers of St. Francis,*
St. Francis of Assisi

⟨⟩⟩ Repair My House ⟨⟩⟩

*T**he holy ones know: the extraordinary*
nestles in the ordinary. The sacred
shines through the mundane. God
hides his face behind your face and mine, your
infant and your enemy, a lover and a stranger.

When Christ told Francis to rebuild his church,
Francis happened to be sitting in the ruins of San
Damiano, and he took the message literally. It
turns out Christ had a much bigger job in mind:
the general reform of the entire community of
Christian believers, everywhere and for all time.

It was a hot summer day, and the young
Francis was trying his hardest to please his
merchant father by peddling sumptuous fabrics
across the Umbrian countryside. But his heart,
never inclined toward commerce to begin with,
had drifted further and further from material
things and settled unmovably on God.

When he came across an ancient church that
had begun to melt back into the earth, Francis
took refuge from the hot sun inside its cool stone
walls. He stood in front of the altar and gazed
up at the crucifix hanging there. His eyes were

drawn to Christ's eyes, which seemed to be looking
directly into his troubled soul with an expression
of heart-wrenching compassion.

Francis dropped to his knees. *You*, he thought,
*are the one who suffered such terrible persecution
on our behalf. And yet you pour your mercy on me,
who has known only privilege.*

Francis was overcome by a bittersweet wave of
gratitude and sorrow. Still holding Christ's gaze,
he wept.

"Francis." The voice penetrated his tears. He
looked around but quickly realized that the crucified Christ was speaking to him from the cross.
"Francis, repair my house, which, as you can see,
is falling into ruins."

Francis' heart swelled with relief. For the first
time in his life, he had a purpose. He would gather
the materials and the labor and he would rebuild
the church of San Damiano. He leapt to his feet, blessed
himself, and returned to Assisi with a mission.

Through the ordinary task of restoring a sacred
site, Francis became the catalyst for the extraordinary return of the lost brotherhood of Christ to the
forgotten virtue of loving service to the Divine in
one another and in all of creation.

One day when he was seated near the hearth, his linen underclothes caught fire the whole length of his leg without his being aware of it.

He felt the heat, but when one of his companions saw that his clothes were burning and hurried to extinguish them, he said to him, "No, my dearest brother, don't harm our Brother Fire." He did not let them put it out.

The brother ran to find blessed Francis' brother guardian and lead him to the place. They extinguished the flames, but against Francis' will.

He did not even want them to extinguish a candle, a lamp, or fire, as one does when it is no longer needed, so great was his tenderness and pity for that creature. He also forbade the brothers to throw embers or half-burned logs to the winds, as is customarily done: he wanted them to be placed gently on the ground out of respect for him who had created them.

— Thomas of Celano,
from *The Life of St. Francis of Assisi*

Sister Earth, Our Mother

Once when he was sitting in a boat near a port in the lake of Rieti, a certain fisherman who had caught a big fish offered it kindly to him. He accepted it joyfully and kindly, and began to call it Brother.

Then placing it in the water outside the boat, he began devoutly to bless the name of the Lord.

While he continued in prayer for some time, the fish played in the water beside the boat and did not go away from the place where it had been put, until his prayers were finished and the holy man of God gave it permission to leave.

— Thomas of Celano,
from *The Life of St. Francis of Assisi*

Though the Crow, black and frightening, is the antithesis of the dove, Francis' crow, thanks to his master, went to choir with the brothers, ate with them in the refectory, and visited the sick in the infirmary of the friary. He also went with them to Assisi's houses to beg for alms.

When Francis died, the crow languished and would take no food. He refused to leave Francis' tomb and died there from grief and weakness.

— Thomas of Celano,
from *The Life of St. Francis of Assisi*

These creatures minister to our needs every day: without them we could not live; and through them the human race greatly offends the Creator. Every day, we fail to appreciate so great a blessing by not praising as we should the Creator and Dispenser of all these gifts.

— St. Francis of Assisi

When the blessed Francis was going across the lake of Rieti to the hermitage of Greccio, he was sitting in a little boat, when a certain fisherman offered him a waterfowl, that he might rejoice over it in the Lord. The blessed father accepted it joyfully, and opening his hands, he gently told it that it was free to fly away.

But when it did not wish to leave, but wanted to rest there in his hands as in a nest, the saint raised his eyes and remained in prayer.

And returning to himself as from another place after a long while, he gently commanded the bird to go back to its former freedom. So upon receiving this permission along with a blessing, the bird joyfully flew away.

— Thomas of Celano,
from *The Life of St. Francis of Assisi*

Francis was sick of the fighting.
Sick of war being waged in the name
of the Prince of Peace. He left Assisi
and plunged into the lands of the Crusades.

He would demand an audience with the
sultan. He would explain everything, the
merciful teachings of Christ. On behalf of his
Muslim brothers, the sultan would forgive
Francis' Christian brothers. He would be so
moved by the Christian message he would lay
down his own sword and follow Christ.

Malik al-Kamil had heard about the Poor
One of Assisi. Having spent his life immersed
in the mystical teachings of Islam, the sultan
recognized Francis as a fellow Sufi. He would
receive him joyfully, reverently. It would not
take much to awaken his Christian brother,
who would remember his true nature and
embrace Islam.

"As'salaam alaykum," the sultan said to
the friar when Francis entered his tent.
"The peace of God be upon you."

"Alaykum as'salaam," Francis answered, as he had been instructed. "And may his peace also be with you."

Francis knelt before Malik.

"Tell me about your faith," the sultan said. "I want to know everything about that which lights such a heart as yours on fire."

Francis spoke. He spoke in a rush of passion and joy, anguish and acceptance. And Malik listened. He listened with gratitude and respect, with amazement and amusement.

At last, the sultan whispered, "La ilahha, il allah."

To which the friar echoed, "There is no God but God."

"Muhammadah rasulullah," Malik added. "And Muhammad is his messenger."

Francis smiled and said, "And Jesus is his Word made flesh."

The sultan burst out laughing, pulled the poor man of Assisi close, and hugged him first on the left, then on the right.

"I'm afraid today is not my day to become a Christian," Malik said, "though your religion is beautiful."

"Nor will I convert to Islam," Francis said, "though your Prophet seems to understand the teachings of my Lord."

"Thank you for the gift of your wisdom," the sultan said to the friar. "And now I grant you safe passage. You are always welcome to come speak to me and to my people of your faith. Pray for me, Brother Francis."

Try to realize the dignity God has conferred on you.

He created and formed your body in the image of his beloved son, and you are made in his own likeness.

And yet every creature under heaven serves and acknowledges and obeys its Creator in its own way better than you do . . .

— St. Francis of Assisi,
in *The Admonitions, V*

At dawn, when the sun rises, we should praise God, who created Brother Sun for us, and through him gives light to our eyes by day.

And at nightfall everyone should praise God for Brother Fire, by whom he gives light to our eyes in the darkness.

For we are all blind, and by these two brothers of ours God gives light to our eyes, so we should give special praise to our Creator for these and other creatures that serve us day by day.

— St. Francis of Assisi, from *Mirror of Perfection*, 119

One night Francis was roaming the lanes of Assisi. The moon had come up fully round and was suspended in the center of the heavens; the entire earth was floating buoyantly in the air. He looked, but he could see no one standing in the doorways to enjoy this great miracle.

Dashing to the church, he ascended the bell tower and began to toll the bell as though some calamity had taken place. The terrified people

awoke with a start, thinking there must be a
fire, and ran half-naked to the courtyard of San
Ruffino's, where they saw Francis ringing the
bell furiously.

"Why are you ringing the bell?" they yelled at
him. "What's happened?"

"Lift up your eyes, my friends," Francis
answered them from the top of the bell tower.
"Lift up your eyes; look at the moon!"

— Nikos Kazantzakis, *God's Pauper*

Every creature in heaven and on earth and in
the depths of the sea should give God praise and
glory and honor and blessing;

He has borne so much for us and has done
and will do so much good to us;

He is our power and our strength and he
alone is supreme good, he alone most high, he
alone all-powerful, wonderful, and glorious;

He alone is holy and worthy of all praise and
blessing for endless ages and ages.

Amen!

— St. Francis of Assisi, in *Letter to All the Faithful*

One time when Francis was walking with another friar in the Venetian marshes, they came upon a huge flock of birds, singing among the reeds.

When he saw them, the saint said to his companion, "Our sisters the birds are praising their Creator. We will go among them and sing God's praise, chanting the divine office."

They went in among the birds, which remained where they were, making so much noise that the friars could not hear themselves saying the office.

Eventually the saint turned to them and said, "My sisters, stop singing until we have given God the praise to which he has a right."

The birds were immediately silent and remained that way until Francis gave them permission to sing again, after the men had taken plenty of time to say the office and had finished their praises. Then the birds began to sing again, as usual.

— St. Bonaventure,
The Life of Saint Francis

Will there come a day
when the fox, at bay,
may find man's shoulder
his shelter, his boulder?

When will the deer
stand without fear
while man's hand touches
his russet haunches?

When will the snare
return to air
the bright-winged captive
to praise God and live?

Saint Francis, when will
man cease to kill
the shy, and that other—
his shyer brother?

— Francis Frost

When Saint Francis was preaching one day to the people of Trevi, a noisy and ungovernable ass went careening about the square, frightening the people out of their wits.

And when it became clear that no one could restrain him, Saint Francis said to him: "Brother ass, please be quiet and allow me to preach to the people."

When the donkey heard this, he immediately bowed his head and, to everyone's astonishment, stood perfectly quiet.

And the blessed Francis, fearing that people might take too much notice of this astonishing miracle, began saying funny things to make them laugh.

— Brother Tebaldo

Who could ever give expression to the very great affection he bore for all things that are God's? Who would be able to narrate the sweetness he enjoyed while contemplating in creatures the wisdom of their creator, his power and his goodness?

Indeed, he was very often filled with a wonderful and ineffable joy from this consideration while he looked upon the sun, while he beheld the moon, and while he gazed upon the stars and the firmament.

O simple piety and pious simplicity!

Even toward little worms he glowed with a very great love, for he had read this saying about the Savior: "I am a worm, not a man." Therefore he picked them up from the side of the road and placed them in a safe place, lest they be crushed by the feet of the passersby.

— Thomas of Celano,
from *The Life of St. Francis of Assisi*

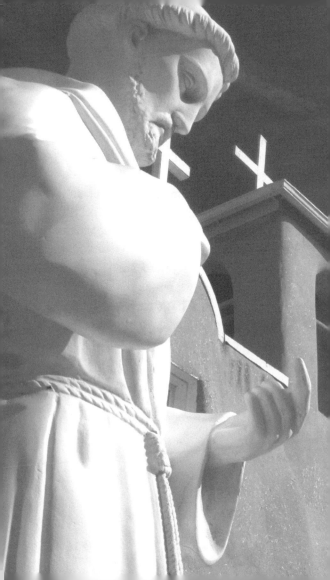

Chapter Two

Honey-Sweet Power

⚭ Vessel of Mercy ⚭

*T*he only truth Francis knows is the lovingkindness of God.

He identifies with Mary as the womb from which Christ, the embodiment and expression of divine love, is born and born again into this world. Like Mary, Francis makes of himself a vessel for mercy and compassion.

Every act is a prayer: Lord, make me an instrument of your peace. Any failure to act lovingly is a shattering of the vessel. With each new act of charity, the container is repaired and restored to wholeness.

He lifts a worm from the road so a passing donkey cart will not crush the Creator's humblest creature. He matches his prayers to the rhythms of the cricket outside his window. He not only washes the wounds of the lepers; he forgives the offenses of the Church hierarchy. He reforms through love, never criticism.

He is not from the lineage of the screaming prophet. He is from the circle of the silent holy ones who heal through being invisible. He empties himself of himself, and this is how he changes the world.

May the fiery and honey-sweet power
of your love, O Lord,
wean me from all things under heaven,
so that I may die
for love of your love,
you who were so good as to die
for love of my love.

— St. Francis of Assisi

⟨∞⟩ Instrument of Your Peace ⟨∞⟩

Lord, make me an instrument of your peace.
Where there is hatred, let me sow love;
Where there is injury, pardon;
Where there is friction, union;
Where there is error, truth;
Where there is doubt, faith;
Where there is despair, hope;
Where there is darkness, light;
Where there is sadness, joy.

O Divine Master,
Grant that I may not so much seek
to be consoled as to console,
to be understood as to understand,
to be loved as to love.

For it is in giving that we receive.
It is in pardoning that we are pardoned.
It is in dying that we are born to eternal life.

— St. Francis of Assisi

A person really loves her enemy when she is not offended by the injury done to herself, but for love of God feels burning sorrow for the imperfection her enemy has brought on his own soul, and proves her love in a practical way.

— St. Francis of Assisi, in *The Admonitions*, IX

When a person envies his brother the good that God says or does through him, it is like committing a sin of blasphemy, because he is really envying God, who is the only source of every good . . .

— St. Francis of Assisi, in *The Admonitions*, VIII

St. Paul tells us, the letter kills, but the spirit gives life. A person has been killed by the letter when he wants to know quotations only so that people will think he is very learned . . . when he has no desire to follow the spirit of Sacred Scripture, but wants to know what it says only so that he can explain it to others.

On the other hand, those have received life from the spirit of Sacred Scripture who, by their words and example, refer to the most high God, to whom belongs all good, all that they know or wish to know, and do not allow their knowledge to become a form of self-complacency.

— St. Francis of Assisi, in *The Admonitions*, VII

When you have stabilized your heart in right faith, and steadfast hope, and perfect love, then you will heave up your heart in high contemplation of your Creator.

— St. Francis of Assisi

☙ Embracing the Wound ☙

What is it within yourself that horrifies you? Can you gently resist the urge to turn away and instead allow yourself to turn toward it? Can you not only face that which repulses or frightens or offends you, but embrace it? Can you let yourself be irrevocably transformed by the encounter?

Early in his awakening, Francis, who was raised with wealth and privilege, crossed paths with a leper. The man's face was eroded by disease, his sores oozing. With the help of two sticks, he hobbled on the rotten stumps of his feet, dutifully clanging his clapper to warn passersby of his proximity.

That day, before Francis had a chance to register the sound, he found himself face-to-face with the leper. Everything in him wanted to run. Revulsion rose in his belly like bile, and his heart thundered in his chest. He drew a deep breath.

"Good morning, brother," he said.

Then he walked up to the man and took his ravaged hands in his own. He brought them to

*his lips and kissed them, then released his hands
and pulled the astonished leper into a close
embrace. He stroked the man's sparse hair.*

*A powerful wave of love washed away
any traces of horror. What was ugly became
unspeakably beautiful. Francis saw no difference between this man's physical wounds, the
suffering of humanity, or Francis' own shattered
heart. No difference between deep sorrow and
profound joy. Compassion and gratitude.*

*Francis never again turned away from bro-
kenness, in other creatures, or in himself.*

*Can you embrace the one inside you whom
you were taught to disdain? Can you invite the
banished one home?*

"Humility is the recognition of the truth about
God and ourselves."

— St. Francis of Assisi

Humility, the guardian and ornament of all the
virtues, had superabundantly filled Francis . . .
He thought of himself as nothing but a transgres-
sor, when in truth he was a mirror shining with
all the reflections of holiness.

Like the wise builder he had learned about
from Christ, he wanted to build his own edifice on
the foundation of humility.

The Son of God, he used to say, left the womb
of the Father and descended from heaven's
heights into our misery to teach us by word and
example . . . what humility is.

Therefore he strove, as Christ's disciple, to
humble himself in his own eyes and those of
others . . .

— St. Bonaventure, from *The Life of St. Francis of Assisi*

You are holy,
O my Lord and only God,
mysterious and holy,
holy and amazing!

You are mighty, magnificent, transcendent.
You are all-powerful,
O most holy Creator,
beneficent ruler of heaven and earth.

You are manifold and One at the same time,
Lord God.
You are utterly wonderful.
You are wonderful, perfectly wonderful,
the very essence of all that is most wonderful,
O Lord God!
You are real and alive.

You are generosity and wisdom,
humility and patience,
safety and serenity,
ecstasy and delight.

You are righteousness and balance,
prosperity that surpasses all basic needs,
you are harmony and beauty.

You are my protector, guardian, and defender.
You are my strength.
You are my sustenance and my courage.

You are faith, hope, and charity.
You are my deepest tenderness.
You are everlasting vitality.

O supreme and marvelous Lord,
Almighty God,
Beloved redeemer,
You are absolute mercy.

— St. Francis of Assisi

Blessed is the person who treasures up for paradise all the favors God has given him and does not want to show them off for what he can get out of them.

God himself will reveal his works to whomever he pleases.

Blessed is the person who keeps God's marvelous things to himself.

—St. Francis of Assisi, in The Admonitions, XXVIII

Nothing, then, must keep us back, nothing
separate us from him, nothing come between us
and him.

At all times and seasons, in every country and
place, every day and all day, we must have a true
and humble faith, and keep him in our hearts,
where we must love, honor, adore, serve, praise
and bless, glorify and acclaim, magnify and thank,
the most high supreme and eternal God . . .

Without beginning and without end, he is
unchangeable, invisible, indescribable and ineffable, incomprehensible, unfathomable, blessed
and worthy of all praise.

— St. Francis of Assisi, in Rule of 1221, Ch. XXIII

The peace you proclaim with words must dwell even more abundantly in your hearts.

Do not provoke others to anger or create scandal. Rather, let your gentleness draw them to peace, goodness, and harmony.

This is our vocation: to heal wounds, to bind what is broken, to bring home those who are lost.

— St. Francis of Assisi,
from *Legend of the Three Companions*

Hail, Queen Wisdom! The Lord is within you,
    and within your sister, pure, holy
    Simplicity.
Lady Holy Poverty, God is in you,
    and in your sister, holy Humility.
Lady Holy Love, God is with you,
    and with your sister, Holy Surrender.

All holy virtues,
    God is within you,
    God, from whom you proceed and come.

There is not a single person in the whole
    world
       who can possess any one of you
       without first dying to herself.

The person who practices one
       and does not violate the others,
       possesses all.
The person who violates one
       possesses none and violates all.

Each and every one of you transcends vice
       and error.

Holy Wisdom transcends the spirit of evil
       and unravels all its tricks.

Pure and Holy Simplicity transcends all the
       learning of this world,
       and surpasses all natural wisdom.

Holy Poverty transcends all greed, clinging,
       and all the anxieties of this life.

Holy Humility transcends pride,
  and all the inhabitants of this world,
  and all that is in the world.

Holy Love transcends all the temptations of
  the spirit of evil
  and of the physical body and overcomes
  all natural fear.

Holy Surrender transcends all ordinary and
  selfish desires.
It quells our lower nature
  and makes us answer to the spirit
  and serve each other.
This level of submission subjects us to
  everyone on earth,
and not only to human beings,
  but to all the creatures as well
  and to the wild animals,
so that they can do what they like with us,
  as far as God allows them.

— St. Francis of Assisi

*A*s he felt the approach of his impending death, Francis climbed to the remote summit of Mount La Verna. It was almost Michaelmas, the forty days between the feast of the Assumption of the Virgin Mary and the feast of Michael the Archangel. St. Michael's Lent, during which summer gives way to fall and creation drops her rich robes and stands naked before her Creator.

Francis wanted to honor this time by fasting, praying, and contemplating the divine passion. He wanted to feel Christ's suffering in his own ravaged body before he left this world behind. He wanted to participate in the perfect love that engulfed Christ's heart in holy fire.

Francis retired to a rocky cave in solitude and silence. That is, except for when Brother Leo would deliver a jug of water and a hunk of bread at daybreak and then join him for prayers at midnight. As Leo approached the hermit's cave, he would call out the opening lines of the evening prayer: "Lord, open my lips!" Francis would answer with the rest of the verse: "And my mouth will proclaim your praise!" If the saint did not respond, that was Leo's signal to leave him alone.

It was the eve of the feast of the Flowering Cross. Francis was kneeling in prayer outside the entrance to his cave in the hour before dawn. As he contemplated Christ's sacrifice, his heart became so enkindled that it burst into flame. Suddenly, it was as if the whole mountain was ablaze. To the shepherds nearby, it seemed that the forest was on fire, and they rushed their sheep down the mountainside. The light was so brilliant that people in the valley below believed that dawn had broken, and began to rouse their families. Brother Leo, who had been spying on Francis from behind a pine tree, saw a ball of fire tumble from the heavens onto his master's head.

Francis looked up into the eyes of a fiery six-winged seraph that was descending swiftly through the sky. Two wings covered its face, two wrapped around its body, and with the other two, it hovered in the air before him. When Francis looked closely, he saw that the *angel bore the form of the crucified Christ. Its expression radiated a heartbreaking blend of anguish and lovingkindness. From the wounds in its feet, hands, and side, the Christ-angel issued beams of light directly into Francis' feet, hands, and side.*

In the morning, Francis bore the wounds of the crucified Christ in his own flesh. Although he tried to hide them, these signs of his mystical union with his savior burned and bled throughout the remaining two years of his life.

The brothers and sisters must guard the times of private prayer with relentless watchfulness.

They must remember that communal worship is not a substitute for the quiet communion of the individual soul with God.

— *The Principles*

Blessed Mother Mary,
You are utterly unique among women:

lover to the King of Kings,
consort of the Creator of all that is,
mother of the most adorable Christ-child,
closest companion to the Holy Spirit.

Will you please convey my praise
to your brave and noble son?

Glory to you, holy woman of God!
Glory to you, perfect one!
Mother of the divine!
The heavenly father chose you as his bride.
In appreciation,
He gifted you with the presence of his sacred son
and the pure dove, everlasting spirit of God.

You are the embodiment of all virtue,
mercy and lovingkindness.
We bow at your feet, O Temple of the Holy One!
You are God's home, his beauty, his beloved!
Praise to you, mother of all!

We adore you.
Through the grace of the Holy Spirit,
You fill our hearts with divine light.
You transform us from faithless souls
to faith-filled children of God.

— St. Francis of Assisi

How St. Francis Teaches Us
⟳ to Open Heaven ⟳

When I was a boy, I thought that heaven
must start behind the stars, their lights
holes in the night that covered God like
    curtains.
There had to be a secret cord that drew them,
revealing God's apartments.

St. Francis
said an enemy's hand was creased with
codes that told the merest boy how to
open God's bright heaven.

The hidden handle
was the enemy's very hand, and
hateful eyes were openings to glory.

But how was I to know what lightless
    labyrinths
those creases trace, how long it takes to
travel easy there before the handle turns.

— Murray Bodo

⟡ **Brother Leo's Blessing** ⟡

The Lord bless you and keep you.
May he show his face to you
and have mercy.
May he turn his countenance to you
and give you peace.

— St. Francis' blessing to Brother Leo,
his closest companion

Chapter Three
Francis and Clare

∽ Mirror of Love ∽

*T*heir love story is as intimate as any, and more succulent than most. They loved each other with heartbreaking passion until the day Francis died, yet they remained celibate. Their love for each other was no more, no less, than a mirror of their love for the Source of All Love.

Clare gave up everything to be with Francis, to live as he lived, to see the face of the Divine in the faces of the poor and the oppressed and to love them as he loved them. "Her goal in life," says Robert Ellsberg about St. Clare, "was not to be a reflection of Francis but to be, like him, a reflection of Christ."

While Francis guided his growing order of Little Brothers, he assigned Clare as the leader of the Poor Ladies.

When Francis felt most alone in the world, most persecuted and misunderstood, it was Clare he would turn to for clarity, wisdom, and a love stripped of sentimentality. "All I want is to live as a hermit and love my Lord in secret," he confessed to her. "And yet I am moved to preach the gospel of holy poverty in the world. What should I do?"

Clare did not equivocate: "God did not call you for yourself alone, but also for the salvation of others."

Toward the end of his life, when the brotherhood had burgeoned so quickly that it threatened to implode, Francis' physical health mirrored the disease spreading through his community. Wracked by unrelenting pain in his joints and flesh, and nearly blind, the forty-six-year-old ascetic took refuge in a hermitage adjoining the convent of the Poor Clares at San Damiano.

There, near to the woman who knew his soul and loved him with a perfect love, and enfolded in the sacred sounds and smells of the creation, Francis composed his ecstatic hymn, "The Canticle of The Sun."

When Francis could no longer hide the grav-
ity of his condition, the brothers took him home
to die. Clare immediately became seriously ill,
sharing the suffering of her beloved in her own
body. When Francis heard that Clare was sick
with grief, he sent her a message.

"I promise, " he wrote, "you will see me
again before you die."

A few days later, the brothers carried
Francis' lifeless body to the cloistered convent
of San Damiano and stopped beneath Clare's
window. They lifted him high so that Clare
could almost reach out and touch his hair. The
friars stood there for as long as Clare wished,
while she filled her eyes with him and wailed.

Clare lived for another twenty-seven years
without her "pillar of strength and consolation,"
yet content in the arms of their common mother,
"Our Lady, Most Holy Poverty." She became a
great and beloved spiritual leader, whose pri-
mary teaching was her life of radical simplicity
and quiet joy.

O how beautiful, how splendid, how glorious did he appear in the innocence of his life, in the simplicity of his words, in the purity of his heart, in his love for God, in his fraternal charity, in his ardent obedience, in his peaceful submission, in his angelic countenance!

He was charming in his manners, serene by nature, affable in his conversation, most opportune in his exhortations, most faithful in what was entrusted to him, cautious in counsel, effective in business, gracious in all things.

He was serene of mind, sweet of disposition, sober in spirit, raised up in contemplation, zealous in prayer, and in all things fervent.

He was constant in purpose, stable in virtue, persevering in grace, and unchanging in all things.

He was quick to pardon, slow to become angry, ready of wit, tenacious of memory, subtle in discussion, circumspect in choosing, and in all things simple.

He was unbending with himself, understanding toward others, and discreet in all things.

— Thomas of Celano, from *The Life of St. Francis of Assisi*

Francis embodies the Gospel journey from violence to non-violence, wealth to poverty, power to powerlessness, selfishness to selfless service, pride to humility, indifference to love, cruelty to compassion, vengeance to forgiveness, revenge to reconciliation, war to peace, killing enemies to loving enemies. More than any other Christian, he epitomizes discipleship to Jesus . . .

Francis' logic points the way toward personal, social and global justice, and peace. If each one of us practiced Gospel simplicity, voluntary poverty, and downward mobility, like Francis, we would share the world's resources with one another, have nothing to fear from others, and live in peace with everyone.

— Father John Dear

She followed him because she loved the treasure. She heard him speak of what he had found, and a passage in her own heart opened up. They had found the same treasure in different caves, and they would share it with whomever they met in that sacred place below the surface of life.

She was Clare and he was Francis, and together they would show the world its hidden heart.

— Murray Bodo

The Elopement

She slips away from her father's house late at night. Not through the front entrance, but through the side door, the hidden passageway reserved for the removal of the dead from the home where they had lived.

This is a kind of death: Clare is leaving the only world she has known and she will never return.

Her bare feet fly through the sleeping streets of Assisi and she vaults over the city walls. He is waiting for her, surrounded by his brothers: Francis, the man she loves with a fire inseparable from her love of God, the two flames entwined.

Clare is all about fire—fire and light—in Italian, Chiara: *clear light.*

The brothers are carrying flaming torches to receive her. "Welcome, Chiara," says Francis.

They lead her through the Portiuncula Forest to the small church of St. Mary's. In a clearing beside the church, Clare professes herself as follower of Francis, lover of Christ, and servant of the Absolute.

With this vow, Clare joyfully relinquishes all that she has been groomed to inherit: wealth, privilege, comfort. All she wants is to embrace a simplicity so naked, there will be nothing left to separate her soul from the Spirit of the Holy One.

As a sign of her renunciation, the beautiful Clare offers her beautiful hair. By the blazing torchlight, Francis himself tenderly lifts each glimmering tress and cuts it. When the shearing is complete, Clare steps out of her embroidered gown and into the rough robe worn by the brothers. Francis tenderly fits the veil of Christ's Bride on her naked head.

Her exultation is as wild as his. Not touching, Francis and Clare circle each other like

*dancers, their eyes shooting flames, laughter
bubbling up from their depths and spilling over
in riotous shouts of joy.*

*What is my father's house, the house that
imprisons me with comfort and ease? What is
the long hair that shields me from the beauty of
this wounded world? What am I willing to let go
of? What kind of letting go would set me free?*

Whenever he spoke, prayed, or thought he was
alone, his squat body shot forth flames that
reached the heavens: he became an archangel
with red wings that he beat in the air.

And if this happened at night when the
flames were visible, you recoiled in terror to keep
from being burned.

"Put yourself out, Brother Francis," I used to
cry. "Put yourself out before you burn up
the world."

— Nikos Kazantzakis, *God's Pauper*

Saint Francis of Assisi

At times when [Brother Giovanni] would hear his master speak of God, his heart would melt like wax near a fire; and the love of God so inflamed him that he was not able to stand still and endure it.

He would get up and, as if drunk in spirit, would go about now through the garden, now through the woods, now through the church, talking as the flame and the impetus of the spirit moved him.

— *The Little Flowers of St. Francis of Assisi*

St. Francis went behind the altar and began to pray. In that prayer he received a divine visitation that inflamed his soul with such love of holy poverty that from the color of his face and the frequent opening of his mouth it seemed as if flames of fire came from him.

Coming toward his companion as if aflame, he cried out, "Ah, ah, ah! Brother Masseo, come to me!" He repeated this three times, and the third time lifted Brother Masseo into the air with his very breath, and propelled him the distance one could hurl a spear.

Brother Masseo . . . later told his companions
that when he had been raised by the saint's breath
and so softly thrown, he had felt such sweetness
of soul and consolation of the Holy Spirit as he
had never felt before or since.

— *The Little Flowers of St. Francis of Assisi*

⟨⟨⟨ Eating Fire ⟩⟩⟩

"*A*ll I ask is to share a meal with you,
Father," Clare pleaded when Francis
visited her at San Damiano.

"*It's not so simple, sister.*"

"*What could be more simple than sharing
a loaf of bread, a handful of raisins, some boiled
carrots? A dozen times I have asked
you. A dozen times you have refused. Why?*"

"*Please, Clare.*" *There was anguish in his
voice.* "*Do not ask me again.*"

*Boldly, she reached for his hands and drew them
to her. He pulled them back as if her hands were
vipers. She turned away, her eyes blinded by tears.*

Later, his companions pressed him. "Father Francis, why are you so strict with her? She has given up everything to follow the path God has shown you. Her wealth and privilege. Her beautiful hair. Physical intimacy. Her love is pure. Why won't you eat with her? This small thing would be so consoling to her."

"It is not the purity of Clare's love I don't trust," Francis admitted. "It's my own."

But the brothers persisted and Francis finally relented. Knowing that Clare had been cloistered for a long time, Francis arranged a meal to be served at Saint Mary of the Angels, where Clare had first cut off her long golden curls as a sign of her pledge of devotion to Lady Poverty.

When the day of her meal with Francis arrived, the brothers escorted Clare to Saint Mary's. She prostrated herself before the altar of the Blessed Mother and lay still for a long time. Finally, the brothers lifted her to her feet and led her outside where Francis had prepared a simple lunch and laid it on the bare ground.

As they sat down to eat, Francis began to speak about God. He held an olive in his hand,

*but it never reached his lips. Clare picked up
a cup of water and immediately put it down
again. Their knees were almost touching. Their
faces were luminous. The companions stood
nearby in reverent silence.*

*The people of Assisi glanced toward the for-
est where St. Mary's was nestled. Flames leapt
from the tops of the trees.*

*"Fire! Fire!" they yelled. Someone rushed up
the bell tower and sounded the alarm. Others
filled buckets, loaded them onto donkeys, and
raced toward the conflagration.*

*But when they burst into the clearing where
the church stood, nothing was burning.*

*Nothing but the hearts of Francis and Clare,
who sat together in divine rapture, their tongues
silenced by grace, their eyes lifted toward the
invisible realm from which the holy fire came.*

*When the blessed meal was over, Clare, who
had eaten nothing, left more satisfied than she
had ever been in her life. So filled that she was
never hungry again.*

*But Francis was overcome with sweet empti-
ness, an emptiness that consumed him until the
day he died.*

༃༚ St. Francis of Assisi ༃༚

Would I might wake St. Francis in you all,
Brother of birds and trees, God's Troubadour,
Blinded with weeping for the sad and poor:
Our wealth undone, all strict Franciscan men,
Come, let us chant the canticle again
Of mother earth and the enduring sun.
God make each soul
the lonely leper's slave:
God make us saints, and brave.

— Vachel Lindsay

Beloved sisters, we must consider the immense
gifts that God has bestowed on us, especially
those he has seen fit to work in us through his
beloved servant, our blessed father Francis . . .

In fact, almost immediately after his
conversion, when he had neither brothers nor
companions, while he was building the church
of San Damiano, where he was totally visited
by divine consolation and compelled to com-
pletely abandon the world, through the great

joy and enlightenment of the Holy Spirit, the holy man made a prophesy about us that the Lord has fulfilled.

For at that time, climbing the wall of that church, he shouted in French to some poor people who were standing nearby:

"Come and help me in the work of building the monastery of San Damiano, because ladies are yet to dwell here who will glorify our heavenly Father . . . by their celebrated and holy manner of life."

We can consider in this, therefore, the abundant kindness of God to us. Because of his mercy and love, he saw fit to speak these words through his saint about our calling.

— from *St. Clare's Testament*

Lady Clare related how once, in a vision, it seemed to her that she brought a bowl of hot water to Saint Francis along with a towel for drying his hands.

She was climbing a very high stairway, but was going very quickly, almost as though she were going on level ground.

When she reached Saint Francis, the saint bared his breast and said to the Lady Clare, "Come, take and drink."

After she had sucked from it, the saint admonished her to imbibe once again. After she did so, what she had tasted was so sweet and delightful she could in no way describe it.

After she had imbibed, that nipple or opening of the breast from which the milk came remained between the lips of the blessed Clare. After she took in her hands what remained in her mouth, it seemed to her it was gold so clear and bright that she saw everything in it as in a mirror.

— Carol Lee Flinders

Place your mind before the mirror of eternity!
Place your soul in the brilliance of glory!
Place your heart in the figure of the divine
　　substance!
And transform your entire being into the
　　image
of the Godhead itself through contemplation.

— Carol Lee Flinders

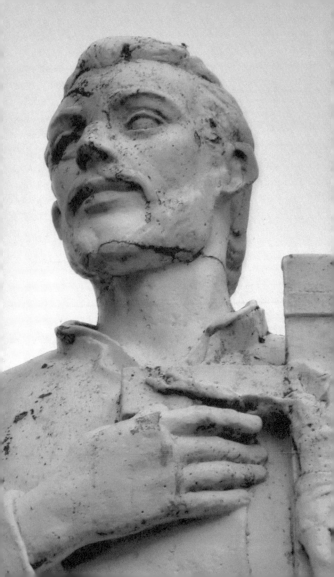

Chapter Four

Little Poor One

*E*very act of renunciation brings Francis closer to the world. By stripping away the protective layer of his own desires, he comes into direct contact with the Source of all satisfaction. By graciously declining the gift of mundane marriage and taking Lady Poverty as his bride instead, Francis falls in love with All That Is.

Detachment from the clamoring lure of consumption does not render Francis stark or severe. It blesses him with deep stillness, so he can hear the lovesong of the Holy One. The deeper the quietude he cultivates, the more the divine music resounds through his soul, echoing into every chamber of his life. Anyone who comes into contact with him can hear it in the air all around him, like the hum of bees sometimes, at other times like a parade coming down fast from the mountain.

Like the Buddha before him, Francis was born into a life of wealth and privilege. He, too, was sheltered from the very real destitution in which the vast majority of people lived. And, like that great saint of India, Saint Francis managed to break away from the cocoon that shielded him from the suffering of other beings and, once having glimpsed their pain, dedicated the rest of his life to alleviating it.

Must he suffer to know God? Must any one of us? Francis' body, never robust, has been devastated by his harsh lifestyle. Self-inflicted penances have so weakened his constitution that he has made himself host to a stunning array of diseases, both common and rare. He suffers from degenerative blindness, so beauty of nature he once so passionately adored has become a memory. The Order of Friars Minor, which he never meant to found, has grown so quickly that it rages out of control, wracked by internal conflict, succumbing to the curse of all holy teachings: institutionalization. The founder has become the target of his followers' discontent. Francis is terribly misunderstood.

And yet, through these tribulations, Francis is able to identify with his Brother Jesus, who endured the ultimate anguish for love of all humanity. Francis' persecution and deprivation allow him to see himself in the outcasts to whose care he is so devoted, and to see in their innocent faces the face of his Beloved.

In spite of his own struggles, Francis continues to tend lepers with loving care, telling them jokes to light their eyes and promising them a magnificent reward for their trials. He still wakes every morning to an explosion of birdsong, and his heart fills with wild joy. He blames no one for his misery. Whenever he begins to slip into the illusion of self-pity, he slaps his own cheeks to reawaken himself to the sheer beauty of life.

It does not take long before the troubadour of God is singing again.

When he was alone . . . his tears began to flow. He would beat his chest, roll in the thorns and nettles, lift his hands to heaven and cry,

"All day long I search for you desperately, Lord; all night long while I am asleep you search for me. O Lord, when, when, as night gives way to day, shall we meet?"

— Nikos Kazantzakis,
God's Pauper

Jesus in agony in the Garden of Gethsemane and Mary in agony somewhere in Jerusalem, unable to do anything, having to stand helplessly by and let her only son suffer the terrible inner struggle that no one else can suffer for us.

Such was St. Francis' feeling, his compassion for Christ . . . He wanted somehow to suffer with Jesus, and so, two years before he died, this prayer rose from the depths of his love . . .

"O Lord, I beg of you two graces before I die—to experience personally and in all possible fullness the pains of your bitter passion, and to feel for you the same love that moved you to sacrifice yourself for us."

— St. Francis of Assisi,
from *The Little Flowers of St. Francis of Assisi*

Joy fall to thee,
Father Francis,
Drawn to the life
that died;
with the gnarls of
the nails in thee,
niche of the lance,
his Lovescape
crucified
And seal of his
seraph — arrival!

— Gerard Manley Hopkins, in
"The Wreck of the Deutschland"

≈≈≈ Naked before God ≈≈≈

*A*fter Christ spoke to Francis from the
ruins of San Damiano, directing him
to rebuild his Church, Francis reached
for the most immediate source of funds available: his father's fabrics. Francis entered Pietro
Bernardone's warehouse when his father was
away on business and helped himself to two
bolts of expensive cloth.

Francis rode to a nearby village, where he sold
both the fabric and his horse. Pocketing his purse
of gold, he set off on foot for the crumbled church
of San Damiano, where he handed the money to
the astonished priest. "This should be enough to
rebuild this house of God," Francis said.

But Bernardone's wrath was infamous, and
the priest had no interest in incurring it. He
refused the money.

When Francis' father returned to Assisi and
discovered what his errant son had done now, he
predictably exploded. He had endured Francis'
outrageous disregard for his hard-earned wealth
long enough.

In Francis' youth, the boy had squandered entire fortunes on entertaining himself and his friends. His father had spent a huge sum to bail him out when Francis was captured as a prisoner of war. He had allowed Francis to do nothing for two years as he recovered from an illness contracted during his incarceration. And now this: stealing from his own father to pursue some crazy new whim.

Bernardone found his estranged son, dressed in rags, begging in the streets of Assisi for stones to rebuild the church of San Damiano. He dragged Francis before the town consul, demanding that the civic officials preside over a disinheritance hearing. But the consul insisted it was a matter for the bishop to adjudicate, since it involved a sum of money donated to the Church. Furious, Bernardone thrashed Francis in the public square.

Francis left his father's house and spent his days and nights praying in a cave outside the city walls, finding refuge in the womb of the earth.

When he was summoned before Bishop Guido, Francis went willingly, considering the bishop to be a representative of God. Guido, known for his violent temper, was surprisingly tender with the recalcitrant young man of God. He tried to reason with him, explaining that he had "scandalized" his father and that God wouldn't want him to use ill-gotten gains to do his work.

"My son," said the bishop, "have confidence in the Lord and act courageously . . . He will be your help and will abundantly provide you with whatever is necessary . . ."

These words penetrated Francis' heart. Moved by a surge of faith, Francis stripped off his clothes in front of the entire assembly and handed them to his father, along with the purse of gold the priest at San Damiano had refused.

"Listen, everyone," Francis called out to the crowd that had gathered to observe the trial. "From now on, I can say with complete freedom, 'Our Father who art in Heaven.' Pietro Bernardone is no longer my father."

Stunned, the bishop wrapped his own cloak around Francis' naked shoulders. His father left the cathedral defeated. This is not the way Bernardone hoped things would work out. What *he really wanted was to have his son back. But Francis, released into the service of humanity, was lost to him forever.*

The whole point about Saint Francis of Assisi is that he certainly was ascetical, and he certainly was not gloomy.

As soon as ever he had been unhorsed by the glorious humiliation of his vision of dependence on the divine love, he flung himself into fasting and vigil exactly as he had flung himself furiously into battle. He had wheeled his charger clean round, but there was no halt or check in the thundering impetuosity of his charge.

There was nothing negative about it; it was not a regimen or a stoical simplicity of life. It was not self-denial merely in the sense of self-control. It was as positive as a passion; it had all the air of being as positive as pleasure. He devoured fasting as a man devours food. He plunged after poverty as men have dug madly for gold.

— G.K. Chesterton, "The Ungloomy Ascetic"

Little Poor One

One morning about the Feast of the Exaltation of the Holy Cross, while he was praying on the mountain-side, Francis saw a seraph with six fiery wings coming down from the highest point in the heavens. The vision descended swiftly and came to rest in the air near him.

Then he saw the image of a man crucified in the midst of the wings, with his hands and feet stretched out and nailed to a cross. Two of the wings were raised above his head and two were stretched out in flight, while the remaining two shielded his body.

Francis was dumbfounded at the sight and his heart was flooded with a mixture of joy and sorrow. He was overjoyed at the way Christ regarded him so graciously . . . but the fact that he was nailed to a cross pierced his soul with a sword of compassionate sorrow.

He was lost in wonder at the sight of this mysterious vision . . . Eventually he realized by divine inspiration that God had shown him this vision in order to let him see that, as Christ's lover, he would resemble Christ crucified perfectly, not by physical martyrdom, but by the fervor of his spirit.

As the vision disappeared, it left his heart ablaze with eagerness and impressed upon his body a

miraculous likeness. There and then, the marks
of the nails began to appear on his hands and
feet, just as he had seen them in his vision of the
man nailed to the cross . . .

— St. Bonaventure, *The Life of St. Francis of Assisi*

O Lord,
when the world was growing cold,
in order that the hearts of human beings
might burn anew
with the fire of your love,
you reproduced the stigmata
of Christ's passion
in the flesh
of the most blessed Francis.

Be mindful
of his merits and prayers;
and in your mercy
grant us the grace
to carry his cross always
and to harvest worthy fruits
of self-sacrifice.

— adapted from a prayer by Pope Leo XIII, 1885

Sweet Saint Francis,
you used to be acquisitive and shallow,
until your devotion to Christ convinced you
to give everything away for his sake.

Your love for the Crucified One
was so complete
that he manifested himself in your own body
through the imprint of his beautiful wounds.

People are selfish and self-indulgent these days.
We need your secret medicine more than ever,
that inscrutable power that inspires comfortable
    men and women
to give up everything.

Teach us to love the poor,
and to desire to serve them
as if they were Christ himself.

— St. Francis of Assisi

Anyone who wishes to practice perfect poverty must renounce all worldly wisdom and even secular learning, to a certain extent.

Divested of these possessions, he will be able to make the great acts of God his theme and offer himself naked to the embrace of the Crucified.

Anyone who clings to his own opinions in the depths of his heart has not renounced the world perfectly.

— St. Francis of Assisi

There are many people who spend all their time at their prayers and other spiritual practices and discipline themselves by long fasts and so on. But if anyone says as much as a word that implies a reflection on their self-esteem or takes something from them, they are immediately up in arms and annoyed.

These people are not really poor in spirit. A person is really poor in spirit when she forgets herself and loves those who strike her.

— St. Francis of Assisi, in *The Admonitions*, XIV

⟨⟨⟨ To Francis the Poor ⟩⟩⟩

Why should we remember you at all?
Is it because you swooped, like fly to dung
To graze the face that makes my own flesh crawl?

Or are you a fond medieval romance hung
In silk, with wolf and larks, an olive tree,
And Clare enraptured by the song you've sung?

No, we remember you when we are free
To fail and sing, to rail and praise and fall
Down to the paradise of Poverty.

— Father David Denny

⟨⟨⟨ Audience with the Pope ⟩⟩⟩

Pope Innocent III was an enigma.
The pope boldly proclaimed himself the
most powerful man in the world, and
yet he was dedicated to the spiritual value of simplicity. He was determined to rescue the Church from
the clutches of flagrant materialism and return her
to the gospel ideals of simplicity and charity.

Saint Francis of Assisi
108

Innocent made it his mission to quash heresy throughout Europe and was highly intolerant of criticism, and yet he made himself available for an audience with anyone who had a sincere petition to present. So it was that the poor man of Assisi, barefoot and dressed in a tattered robe, his heart on fire with love of God, made his way into the presence of the highest authority in Christendom.

Championed by Guido, the bishop of Assisi, Francis approached the pope for his blessing of the simple rule that he had drafted for his newly formed brotherhood. Wild variations of this encounter abound.

In one, the pope, disgusted by the sight of Francis and his unwashed band of misfits, banished them on the spot, telling Francis to go wallow among the pigs in the pigsty, where he belonged. According to this account, Francis immediately did as he was told, returning to the pope sometime later, reeking of pig dung. The pope was so moved by the friar's obedience that he sanctioned the new monastic order.

In another account, the pope is portrayed not as a power-hungry despot but as a wise and compassionate soul who recognized Francis as a true man of God. In this version, the pope listened with rapt attention to the holy fool and then rose from his throne, his eyes welling with tears, and embraced the ascetic, thanking him for his wisdom and courage.

Most agree that Brother Francis and the Holy Father met at least twice, and that the catalyst for their second meeting was a dream.

During his first audience, Francis presented his case for a Rule of Life based on voluntary poverty and works of charity. The pope was skeptical, deeming the rule too austere. No one could stick with such rigorous demands, he said. The order would wither before it ever had a chance to take root.

Francis insisted that Christ would be their guide and their strength. The pope suggested that he go away and pray that Christ provide him with a more viable vision of reform.

That night, it was not Francis but the pope who was visited with a revelation.

He remembered a dream he had had a few weeks earlier in which he saw himself asleep in his bed, dressed in all his papal finery. He noticed that the walls of the church in which he was resting were leaning at such a precarious angle that they were about to collapse. A small man, poor yet happy, was holding up the structure with his simple wooden staff. The pope recognized Francis as the man in his dream and realized that God had sent the friar to save the Church from tumbling into ruin.

The next day, the pope approved Francis' simple plan for a brotherhood based on the gospel teachings of radical simplicity and social justice. He gave them the mission to preach their teachings of brotherly love throughout the Holy Roman Empire, tending the sick and assisting the poor, rebuilding ruined churches and begging for their basic needs.

Filled with joy, Francis blessed the Holy Father and named him honorary lifetime member of the Order of Little Brothers.

Most lovable Saint Francis,
Patron of merchants,
you have a way of opening everyone's hearts,
transforming personal ambition into charity.

You were born into wealth and privilege,
and yet you gave it all up
to follow the Good Shepherd
and help him gather lambs.
That's how much you loved Him.

People are so greedy these days,
buying and selling for nothing but personal gain.
We need business people who are honest and kind.
Please, fill the hearts of those men and women
with abundant generosity.
Remind them of the only thing that endures:
love for one another.

— Traditional Prayer
adapted by Mirabai Starr

Where there is love and wisdom,
    there is neither fear nor ignorance.
Where there is patience and humility,
    there is neither anger nor annoyance.
Where there is poverty and joy,
    there is neither grasping nor greed.
Where there is peace and contemplation,
    there is neither anxiety nor restlessness.
Where there is awe of God guarding the dwelling,
    there no adversary can enter.
Where there is mercy and moderation,
    there is neither excess nor harshness.

— St. Francis of Assisi, in *The Admonitions*, XXVII

We can never know how patient or humble a person is when everything is going well with him.

But when those who should cooperate with him do exactly the opposite, then we can know.

A person has as much patience and humility as he has then, and no more.

— St. Francis of Assisi, in *The Admonitions*, XIII

Praised be you,
my Lord,
for all those
who pardon one another
for your love's sake,
and endure weakness
and tribulations;

Blessed are they
who peaceably shall endure,
for you,
O most High,
shall give them
a crown.

— St. Francis of Assisi, in "Canticle of the Sun"

ᢍᡃᢍᡃ Ciao Francesco ᢍᡃᢍᡃ

Ciao Francesco of Assisi
whose bloody footprints in winter
(like carnelians cast upon snow)
can still disrupt Assisi

Ciao Francesco of the Porziuncola
that blessed door too narrow
for me to enter, but led by you
I asked three things

Ciao Francesco of San Damiano
who led me along the same
road of renunciation
(while the silver olive trees wept)
and showed me that we
leave all our fathers

Ciao Francesco of the Carceri
whose food was to do the
will of God, and when I
saw this—too true—I ran
all the way down Mount Subasio

Ciao Francesco of the Chiesa Nuova
your lively friar-son showed me
the prison where your father
tried to keep you and then
sensing my sins he let down
his cape for me to walk on
—this still hurts

Ciao Francesco who fought the devils
and guarded my own room with
Leo's cherished blessing—while the
shutters rattled from the nightmare
howls, and the dark dreams
threatened to turn me back

Ciao Francesco of La Verna
(my dearest home)
you climbed those rocks
to bemoan your sins and
left that mountain so transfigured,
so holy, that in that place
I could scarcely breathe

Ciao Francesco of the Basilica
your body is the Feast
Of Fools,
parades, endless masses, cameras, dances,
songs, candles, and those weeping
because they have put you so high,
we can't even touch you
for healing anymore

Ciao Francesco wounded-winter light
you are stricken with love
by God's smallest creatures

Ciao Francesco of the Via Crucis
winter in Assisi is more harsh, silent
and bitter than I ever imagined,
and as I complained and nagged you
for comfort, you walked with me
(like Jesus at Emmaus, wounds aglow)
and taught me the grace of
compassion . . .

— Father William Hart McNichols,
from *Reflections from Assisi*

Little Poor One

Closing Prayer

O Saint Francis,
Little Poor One of Assisi:
your stunning simplicity
lights all my preconceptions of holiness
on fire
and reduces my half-hearted devotion
to ash.

Your lovingkindness
is a lion's roar,
sweeping through the forest
of the human condition,
bringing the mighty to their knees.

Your harmlessness
is a brilliant beacon
guiding my path
to the crossroads where
all the weary and the broken
lay their heads in my lap
and I have nowhere to turn,
no choice but to bend down
and tend them.

Sweet Saint Francis,
teach me to love my enemy
as your brother Jesus taught you.
Show me how to release
self-righteousness
and leave the wicked
to look inside their own hearts.

O you helpless, hopeless lover of God,
show me how to release hope,
relinquish help,
and love God with utter abandon.

Brother of all creation,
let me lift my voice to mingle with yours
in praise of all God's creatures.
I want to claim this place as my place, at last,
include all beings as my family:
rain and rainbow;
mud and cloud,
and the sun breaking through the cloud
and turning the mud into fertile soil;
the tracks of seagulls in sand

and sand and seagulls;
sparrows, wolves;
wild mint and apple seeds;
the placenta of the newborn baby who will
    never know her father,
and the last breath of the grandmother who
    died alone.

Remind me,
wise fool of God,
how to embrace radical simplicity,
knowing that all wealth belongs to the
    Holy One.
Remind me
that he loves me even more than I love him,
and that he wants to give me everything,
everything.
Remind me
that the well-being of all humanity
is the most precious treasure
and give me the courage
to guard it with my life.

Friar Francis,
may your example
show me how to be an example.
May I teach
not through the words of my mind
but through the actions of my heart.
May my life be a light
to guide the lost back to themselves,
home to the loving arms
of the loving God,
to the place where sorrow
is alchemically transformed
by a single drop
of wild joy.

Amen.

— Mirabai Starr

Sources

Page 66-68:   "Hail, Queen Wisdom . . ." from
                www.catholic.org

Page 71:   "The Principles" from *St. Francis
                of Assisi: Writings and Early
                Biographies*

Page 72-73:   Adapted by Mirabai Starr

Page 74:   "How St. Francis Teaches Us to
                Open Heaven" from *Francis: The
                Journey and the Dream*

Page 75:   "Brother Leo's Blessing" from
                *St. Francis of Assisi: Writings and
                Early Biographies*

Page 80:   "The Life of St. Francis of Assisi"
                from *St. Francis of Assisi: Writings
                and Early Biographies*

Page 81:   "Francis embodies the Gospel . . ."
                from *You Will Be My Witnesses*

Page 81-82:   "She followed him . . ." from
                Clare: A Light in the Garden

Page 84:   "Whenever he spoke . . ." from
                God's Pauper

Page 85:   "The Little Flowers of St. Francis of
                Assisi" from *St. Francis of Assisi:
                Writings and Early Biographies*

Page 85-86:   "The Little Flowers of St. Francis of
                Assisi" from *St. Francis of Assisi:
                Writings and Early Biographies*

Bibliography

Books

Bodo, Murray. *Clare: A Light in the Garden.* Cincinnati, Ohio: Saint Anthony Messenger Press, 1979.

Bodo, Murray. *Francis: The Journey and the Dream.* Cincinnati, Ohio: Saint Anthony Messenger Press, 1988.

Chesterson, C.K. *Saint Francis of Assisi.* Garden City, NY: Doubleday Image Books, 1957.

Dear, Fr. John, and William Hart McNichols. *You Will Be My Witnesses.* New York: Orbis Books, 2006.

Fitzgerald, Judith and Michael Oren Fitzgerald, eds. *Christian Spirit.* Indiana: World Wisdom, Inc., 2004.

Flinders, Carol Lee. *Enduring Grace.* New York: HarperCollins, 1993.

Gasnick, Roy M., ed. *The Francis Book.* New York: Macmillian Publishing, 1980.

Habig, Marion A., ed. *St. Francis of Assisi: Writings and Early Biographies.* Chicago: Franciscan Herald Press, 1973.

Hopkins, Gerard Manley. *Mortal Beauty, God's Grace.* New York: Vintage Press, 2003.

Kazantzakis, Nikos. *God's Pauper.* New York: Faber and Faber, 2000.

Ladinsky, Daniel. *Love Poems from God.* New York: Penguin Group, 2002.

Lindsay, Vachel. *General William Booth Enters into Heaven and Other Poems.* NP: Hard Press, 2006.

Mitchell, Stephen, ed. *The Enlightened Heart.* New York: HarperCollins, 1989.

Sister Nan. *The Message of St. Francis.* New York: Penguin Studio, 1999.

Websites

www.catholic.org

Credits

"Ciao Francesco" by Father William Hart McNichols used by permission of Father William Hart McNichols.

◌৩◌ Art Credits ◌৩◌

Cover/Page xii   Painting of Saint Francis. © Darina Gladišová.

Page xiv   Artist unknown, from page 52 of *The Francis Book* (Compiled and Edited by Roy M. Gasnick, O.F.M.).

Page 30   Print of Saint Francis by Fritz Eichenberg. Art © Fritz Eichenberg Trust / Licensed by VAGA, New York, NY.

Page 53   San Franciso de Asis. © Randall Stevens / Shutterstock.

Page 76   Painting of Saint Clare and Saint Francis. © Darina Gladišová.

Page 94   Statue of Saint Francis. © Shane Thomas Shaw / Shutterstock.

Page 118   Statue of Saint Francis, Enchanted Garden at Edgar Allan Poe Museum, Richmond, Virginia. © Alfred Wekelo / Shutterstock.

A good faith effort was made to discover the copyright holder of each image included. If you have any information about uncredited images, please contact the Sounds True Art Department at (303) 665-3151.

About Sounds True

Sounds True was founded in 1985 with a clear vision: to disseminate spiritual wisdom. Located in Boulder, Colorado, Sounds True publishes teaching programs that are designed to educate, uplift, and inspire. We work with many of the leading spiritual teachers, thinkers, healers, and visionary artists of our time.

To receive a free catalog of tools and teachings for personal and spiritual transformation, please visit www.soundstrue.com, call toll-free 800-333-9185, or write to us at the address below.

SOUNDS TRUE

PO BOX 8010 / BOULDER, CO 80306